Copyright 2023
Aundrya Richardson

Let's Connect!

Thank you for taking time to read this story! I pray you enjoy it and that you will continue to follow my work as a self-published author who desires to change the world through writing! Please leave a review on Amazon at the link below, they mean everything and is always appreciated!

God Bless,
Author Aundrya Richardson

www.amazon.com/author/aundryaschnel
www.amazon.com/author/aundryatheauthor

Podcast – Voice Among the Sheep
Facebook: Aundrya the Author
IG: @aundryatheauthor | @writewithaundrya

Impact Writing LLC
impactwritingllc.square.site

INTRODUCTION

I was on the app Clubhouse one Sunday, and I went into a room that was created to talk about different topics concerning the area of mental health and mental illness. This particular day, the topic was addressing if therapy actually works or if it was a waste of time. The room was packed, everyone had their own opinion and perspective about the topic. I can't remember if I shared anything about my experience or not, but it was in that room that an idea began to stir, and it's the reason that you're reading this book! I drew the conclusion that if someone came to me and said *"Aundrya, does therapy work?" My response would be, "no, it doesn't! Therapy doesn't work, you have to work therapy!"* Now that I have finished this book, that will be my response from now on because it's true! As you see, the title of the book is *"Therapy Won't Work, Until You Work Therapy!"*

I worded the title this way for a reason. When I was in this room on Clubhouse, listening to people share perspectives about the effectiveness of therapy, I started paying close attention to those who were against it. I started paying close attention to those who said that therapy didn't work and that it was a waste of time. I paid attention because the ones who said it didn't work, were ones who tried it themselves and found that it didn't work for them. So, because it didn't work for them, they assumed it was ineffective across the board when it's not true. That was the moment this title and this book came to my mind. I wanted to write a book, guide and tool that helps men and women around the world understand that while therapy may not be for everyone, it serves a purpose! It serves a purpose that is effective, but it's all about the response of the recipient. I didn't know the people who spoke against the effectiveness of therapy, but I believe that the reason they drew the conclusion that therapy didn't work was because they did not know how to work therapy. I'm not a therapist or counselor of any kind, I'm a woman who deals with mental illness. I was diagnosed with Major Depressive Disorder, Bipolar Disorder, Anxiety Disorder, and Post Traumatic Stress Disorder (PTSD). After several years of experience as a recipient of the mental health system, I have reached the place where I can share what I've come to learn with you. I can tell you from my own experience and knowledge that therapy began to work for me, once I learned how to work therapy.

I thank you for taking time to invest in yourself and in your mental health journey by purchasing this book! I believe that by the end of this book, you will have gained knowledge and understanding of how the true effectiveness of therapy is when you know how to work it instead of waiting for someone to make it work for you. My goal is to help you reshape your expectations of what therapy is and what it should be as it pertains to your life. It doesn't matter if you're simply thinking about going to therapy, you're getting ready to go for the first time or you're already actively in therapy. This book will help you if you find yourself in a place where you have mixed feelings about the true purpose and effectiveness as it pertains to you and your journey! That's right, this is all about you! Remember, therapy is not for everyone and I'm not here to say that you have to go or that it's mandatory because it's not. I know a few people personally who have experienced some of the most traumatic events in their life, and they're doing great, and they reached that place of greatness without therapy. They found what worked for their healing and that is okay to do. But for those who want to take advantage of therapy, if you've been feeling uneasy about your decision, I want this book to help you be at peace with your decision.

By the end of this book, it won't matter who says therapy doesn't work because you will have an understanding as well the tools needed to see therapy work in your life, and you continue living life missing out on your own healing because of the opinions of other people who don't see it the way that you do. In other words, therapy is going to work for you because you will work therapy and you will see results!

-Aundrya Richardson

Therapy Won't Work, Until You Work Therapy!

TABLE OF CONTENTS

Remember Your "Why"

Making the choice to go to therapy is not something you just wake up one day and decide to do. If you have reached a place in your life where you realize that you need therapy, there's a reason for it. The question you ask yourself is *"why do I want to go to therapy?"* or *"why do I need therapy?"* Even if it was someone else who came and said that you needed to go to therapy, still ask yourself why you want to go because a decision like this has to be made by you and no one else. Because journaling is a huge part of your journey that I'll be speaking on throughout this book, it is not a bad idea to write that question down for yourself and write down the answers that you come up with.

It will be a good way to remind yourself throughout your healing journey on why you chose to start this process, and this is where we will begin. If you're reading this and you've never been to therapy, but you're at the place where you believe it's time for you to go, ask yourself, *"why am I doing this?"* Ask yourself this question and be honest about it. Did someone tell you to go or did you make the decision on your own? Did you see an ad in the newspaper, on television or online that said you should go to therapy? For this next challenge, please answer those questions below.

Once you've been able to answer that question, ask yourself, *"what has happened in my life to make me realize that I need to go to therapy?"* A wordy question I know, and understand that this is not a question you have to give a lengthy answer to right this moment. You will have plenty of time in therapy to dialogue and expound on different events in your life. It can be as simple as writing down a few key words that categorize what has taken place to make you want to go to therapy. For this next challenge, describe in as much or as little detail what specific event(s) has taken place in your life that has made you realize that you need to go to therapy.

Using myself and my own experience as an example, I would write down things like past trauma, abuse, feeling anxious all the time, crying more often than normal, etc as detailed reasons for why I felt like therapy was going to be an option for me. These are really add-ons to the major event that started my journey in therapy, that major event was the death of my mother. That is something I will talk more in detail about in the book I'll be releasing this June called *Grieving With Purpose*. If you're wondering why you need to be this descriptive, I promise that you will understand this better in the next chapter. Now, here's the question I get asked often by people who are starting out seeking therapy or even counseling. They ask me if they should tell anyone close to them about their decision.

At the end of the day, that decision is up to you, but I personally don't believe you should tell anyone anything. Even if you think they're your closest friend, it could be a spouse, your pastor, a relative, whoever! By keeping your plans for therapy to yourself, you avoid the risk of someone ignorantly saying something to you that could ultimately discourage your decision to seek help and make you rethink the process altogether. However, if you're feeling that you have someone you can trust with the information, then it is okay to share as long as you know the person you tell will be supportive and not judgemental. Judgemental people who choose to remain ignorant about the impact that therapy has instead of doing their own research, are stumbling blocks that will hinder you every step of the way if you allow it. As I stated before, there are people who don't believe in therapy because it didn't work for them, but don't let another person's experience define yours! Taking this first step to seek therapy is big and you should definitely be proud of yourself for doing it because it does take real courage and a level of vulnerability to go to therapy. Don't believe the lies that people say about why you shouldn't go to therapy because in most cases, it's a myth or an opinion that can't be proven. While people are entitled to your opinion, no one has the right to the decision that you make concerning your own life, no matter what.

Again, know your "why" and remember it! As you start or continue the journey of therapy, knowing why you started this journey and remembering why you started is going to be key because it will be what motivates you to stay the course on the good days as well as the bad. I can't say this enough but guard your ears and don't let others' ignorance impact you! Even though I've advised you not to share with everyone about your choice to pursue therapy, it won't stop moments where people around you make negative statements about therapy or people who go to therapy. Understand that not all statements made are directed at you and sometimes you will find yourself in spaces where people will make statements indirectly.

I remember a job I had. I was there one day and one of my coworkers said *"No one needs therapy, I never needed it and I'm fine! I just listened to Gospel music."* At the time that she made this statement, she didn't know that I battled with mental illness. Was I bothered by her statements? Yes, I was! I was very bothered because it was one of the stupidest things I ever heard someone say. But I had to take a deep breath and remember that she's not talking about me, and not to take her words personally.

This is an example of what I mean when you may hear someone make statements ignorantly. Now, there is a line that legally, people are not allowed to cross, especially in spaces like work, church, etc. I'll talk more later in the book about knowing your rights and what your options are when wrong has been done or said against you. On the lines below or in your own journal, name a time where you heard an ignorant or false statement about people who go to therapy. Was it directed at you, or was it spoken indirectly? Did you say something about it? How did it make you feel?

Again, remembering why you chose to go to therapy is key to the success of your journey. As you can see, there are many things that will come to try and deter you from the journey you've chosen, but remembering your "why" is what will push you to ignore the outside negativity by continuing to focus on yourself. In the event that you tell someone about your decision to go to therapy and they begin to question, understand that every statement made doesn't warrant an answer. Some people are better off being left with their thoughts, and when it's a person who you know will believe whatever they want to believe regardless, I wouldn't waste my time trying to explain. The truth is, you don't owe anyone an explanation on how and why you're choosing to take care of your mental health.

Think about this, one of the first things that people say when there's a report of someone killing themselves is telling everyone to seek help! Content like this is to help someone not be driven to the place of hopelessness that causes them to take their own lives because they suffered in silence and were too afraid to seek therapy due to a lack of support or just simply not knowing their options. Now understand, I am not saying that every person who seeks therapy is suicidal. I know that's not always the case at all and if that's not the case for you, great! But for some it is, and I can attest to the fact that the wrong word spoken at the wrong time can be detrimental to that person's life, even if that detriment is just them simply choosing not to get the help they need because of what someone else said. Even though you're not meant to walk this journey alone, there are still many decisions that solely have to be made by you and the decision to go to therapy is one of them. Is making this decision an easy one? Not all the time! It's okay if you struggled to say yes, or maybe you're reading this book and you haven't decided yet. That's okay too, I totally understand and I'm here to be of support on your journey through this book. I hope something that is shared here will help you make the best decision that suits you and no one else! Happy healing and welcome! Your process and journey to true inner healing, wholeness and restoration has already started!

Expect the Unexpected!

Making the decision to go to therapy is one thing, choosing the right therapist for you is another! Establishing a good rapport and level of trust with your new therapist is very important and key in this process. Not everyone who is certified is certified to treat you, remember that. In other words, every therapist is not for everyone and it is okay to take your time in deciding which therapist will be right for you. Now this chapter may sound like it's solely directed as those who have not yet started therapy and are still looking for a therapist, but this information can also apply to those who are already seeking therapy if you find yourself in a place where you're not as happy as you would like to be with your therapist, or if you feel emotionally disconnected from the therapist that you're seeing. It can also help those who stopped going to therapy completely but are thinking about going back again. I'll give an example by talking about myself.

There were times where I talked to a therapist without ever taking time to ask the right questions and establishing that level of rapport and trust with them before I began having sessions with that therapist. While it didn't always turn out bad, there were moments in my journey through therapy where it didn't end on the best note because I was talking to someone who was certified, but they just weren't certified to properly handle what I needed with the amount of care and understanding that it deserved. While moments like that weren't ideal for me, I didn't give up on therapy altogether, I just changed my approach in how I went about choosing the right therapist. So, you may be asking how to go about choosing the right therapist for you and even what questions to ask during the initial consultation. To every process there are steps and what I would encourage you to do first is write down why you're choosing to go to therapy so that you have it as your focal point when preparing yourself for what to look for in a therapist and what questions to ask when you think you've found it. Next, you will write down the things that you've been feeling or experiencing. In no way am I asking you to self-diagnose yourself, but you in your own words, write down what's been happening to you. For example, if you've been hearing voices, write down that you've been hearing voices. If you're sad all the time, write about it! Talk about how often you're and how long you're sad for before your mood shifts again. If you're having trouble controlling your anger, write it down!

Whatever you've been feeling, good, bad or ugly, write it down and don't hold back. What I mean is, don't fear that if you express a certain moment that you're having to the therapist, you're going to be judged or treated a certain way by that therapist. Be totally honest and transparent at this stage so that when you find the right therapist, you can rest assured in knowing you're receiving the best care possible for all of your symptoms. What your therapist doesn't know can't be treated and can have a lasting effect. When I first started counseling, I didn't realize how important it was to establish a good rapport and trust with the therapist, that understanding came much later. Because I wasn't aware of it when I first began my journey, I spent some years going to a counselor every week but never telling her everything that was happening with me when I was alone and I didn't tell her the full story about my symptoms during our sessions. Now understand that it is normal to start therapy and have some topics that you're needing time to work up the courage to talk about, and that is okay to do. You should never pressure yourself or allow anyone to pressure you to share about things that you're not ready to discuss. However, having a therapist that you have a good rapport with and that you have established trust with will make it easier to talk about the hard things when the time is right.

One of the biggest reasons establishing rapport and trust with your therapist before starting your sessions is important, is because in order for therapy to work, you as the client/patient must remain open with your therapist at all times. What I mean is that you have to trust their leadership and not be afraid to follow their directives throughout the process, even when what they instruct you to do seems crazy or irrelevant to where you are. I say this because when you agree to see a therapist, whether it's your very first time or you're returning back to therapy after spending a period of time away from it, you don't know what your process is going to look like. Yes, you know that you desire to heal and live life in a way that you're not held captive to the trauma and pain from your past, but if you had the remedy to see that take place, you wouldn't need a therapist. You wouldn't even need to read this book! But because you came seeking help from a therapist, it is important not to have a preconceived notion about what you believe the steps to healing should look like. It is important that you trust the process from start to finish, even when you're asked to do things that don't seem to make the most sense, trust it and do it! If you do it, you will start to understand as the process continues why your therapist asked you to do some of the things you did. For example, one year my therapist told me that she wanted to put me into a six week program where I would participate in group therapy. I knew what group therapy was but I had never been open to sitting in a room with other people and talking about my struggles.

I just didn't think I could handle it. But based on what I was dealing with at the time, my therapist thought it was best and because I had a great rapport with my therapist and I trusted her, I agreed to it. I struggled at first in the sessions and I felt so much anxiety my first day in group therapy, but over time it changed. I stuck out the process and it changed. I remember being so frustrated at first when the counselors would open every session by having us do breathing exercises because I never practiced breathing and it didn't make sense to me. But I did it and the more I did it, the better I started to feel. By the time I finished those sessions, I was practicing breathing daily and I had a breathing regimen that helped me when I found myself having an anxiety attack. Breathing soon made the difference in how I went through those moments and I still use those techniques today. So again, some therapists will make suggestions based on the individual patient and what they are dealing with at that time. Finding a therapist that you're comfortable with will help you remain open throughout your journey in therapy. If you're seeing a therapist but aren't comfortable with what they suggest for you to do, I would strongly encourage you to find a new therapist who you will connect with in a way that will push you to be open to the process. I say this because refusing to follow your therapist's directives will hinder your growth and journey through therapy and therapy will become ineffective if you're not following the steps that the therapist will ask you to take. So, finding the right one is key.

When you find one that sparks your interest, be sure to verify their credentials and confirm that they are a certified provider for the state you live in. Their profile should list their license number which can be looked up using Google in order to find out where they are licensed. If you don't see one listed, you can call the Department of Health for your state and ask for a directive on how to confirm the validity of a therapist that you're interested in seeing. While I've never been in a situation where I dealt with someone who attempted to practice unlicensed, it happens a lot more than you think, especially among religious organizations. So confirm that information before making your final decision and if you can, utilize your health insurance to help you. Once you've found one, don't be afraid to ask the right questions during your initial consultation so that you're clear on what you can expect from the therapist as it pertains to their approach to therapy.

Trust the Process

I mentioned trusting the process briefly in the last chapter and I wanted to focus on it more in this next chapter because there are other components to consider when going through your process and finding the right therapist is the first because it starts there after making the decision to seek therapy. So again, as a review from what I mentioned in the last chapter, this is what you want to keep in mind when choosing the right therapist to work with on your journey...

1. Do your research on the therapist to make sure their license to practice is real and not fraudulent.
2. Prior to your consultation with the potential therapist, think about what you're looking for in a therapist and what you want to accomplish in therapy. As you do that, write those goals down as well any specific questions you want to ask your therapist so that it helps you make the right decision on who to see.
3. Once you start seeing your therapist, remain open and trust the process! This means that you will do as you're told and you won't be opposed to what your therapist advises you to do because if you are, it will hinder your growth and the sessions will be ineffective.
4. Remember that in trusting the process, you're willing to do what's asked of you in an act of faith. This means that even if you don't know exactly why you're being asked to do

something a certain way, you will still do it with everything you have because you trust the therapist enough to do so. You will find that taking those steps will eventually give you clarity on why it had to be done this way and you will feel a lot better about your progression as you continue your journey.

Before we continue to the next steps of trusting the processes, I want to allow you the chance to release all that you're feeling and thinking after reading this information so far by answering these questions...

1. Have you ever been in therapy before? If yes, why did you stop going? Are you at a place where you want to go back?

2. Are you currently in therapy? If so, has the
    information been of help to you in any way or
    were these things that you considered prior to
    starting therapy?

---

3. What was the driving force that motivated you
    to invest in this book? Be totally honest!

---

4. As you prepare to seek therapy, has the
    information provided so far given you what
    you need when it comes to finding the right
    therapist? Why or why not?

____

____

____

____

5. Are the questions I wrote in this book the
    same questions you plan to ask the therapist
    you want to see? Or do you have a different
    set of questions and expectations for what you
    want?

____

____

____

____

Questions & Expectations For My Potential Therapist

Another component to trusting the process of going through therapy and your journey to healing is your belief system. It is up to you to believe that what you're embarking upon will work for you, even if others don't see it! One thing I strongly encourage to anyone who is new to counseling or even if you've been at it for a while, don't tell everyone what you're doing. Having support is necessary but you must have the right kind of support when walking through a process as delicate as this one. The wrong word spoken at the wrong moment has the power to shift your thinking and make you quit before you ever start or before you reach the finish line. Journaling is a great outlet when expressing how you feel about going to therapy. While there is nothing wrong with telling someone just make sure you tell someone who is graced to support you and not tear you down.

Once you start therapy, you can mention to your therapist that you're in need of a good support system as you start the process, and the therapist can make adequate suggestions for you. The words spoken over you play a part in your belief system which is why I said being mindful of who you talk to is important. Even though you don't know exactly what will happen in therapy and how it will happen, it is still important to believe that what you're looking to get out of therapy will happen for you and allow that to keep you motivated on your journey. I won't lie to you, therapy is rewarding but it's not easy, especially when you've been through any amount of trauma in your past.

I have always encouraged the idea of children going through therapy right after a traumatic experience because the sooner they start the healing, the easier the process to wholeness will be. But everything I share here is mainly for adults like me who for a number of reasons waited until later in life to seek therapy. That being said, going through the process of uprooting deep pain that may have started as early as our childhood, it's not impossible but it does take a lot of work. It comes with the hard questions being asked, questions that help you find your voice by adding the right language to what you've experienced. This goes back to why I said it is important to remain open through the process and to have a therapist that you trust and have a good rapport with.

There may be some pain inside of you that you don't even realize is there until the right questions are asked that will cause you to respond in a way that sheds light to what has remained hidden in the dark places of your spirit. Don't believe the myth that says that it's best not to explore those areas that you may have forgotten about because it will only trigger old pain. The truth is, all deep rooted pain from our past has its way of showing up in our present, even when we don't realize it. It shows up in our interactions with family, friends, coworkers, etc. If you think about it, the pain of your past and how it impacts you today is a large part of why you're at the place of seeking therapy. So, I said all of that to say that exploring every place from your past at the right time during therapy will be hard at certain moments, but it will ultimately pay off in the end when you've healed from it and you start living with assurance that the trauma of your past no longer controls your present or dictate your future. For this last journal for this chapter, allow yourself to be honest and transparent by writing down what fears you have of starting this process through therapy and what you believe it will take to overcome those fears. If you're reading this and you've already started therapy, what were your fears before starting? Do you still have those fears now? If you do, what do you think will help you overcome those fears as you journey with your therapist?

Know Your Rights

Unfortunately, there are many men and women who battle with mental illness are unaware of their rights and the options they have when it comes to certain benefits or knowing what to do when facing opposition related to their illness. Having the right support around you is necessary but there is still responsibility on your end that comes with the care you receive and the way you live your life day to day. There are people in the world who will mistreat and take advantage of people that have mental illness when they believe they can get away with it and when they are convinced that you're incompetent. But people like that only win with those who don't know their rights and that is the purpose for this chapter. I want for every person who reads this book to leave knowing all of their options!

While there are some people who are mentally incapable of making decisions for themselves due to the severity of their illness, that is not the case for everyone! Don't believe anyone who says that mental illness has a look or that someone with mental illness isn't smart or is incapable of taking care of themselves because all of those are myths! There are many people who live with mental illness but you would never know it because they still function in society just like every other person. I am one of those people! I've been told plenty of times that I don't look like I have it because I talk well and I can go to work, school, etc. However, I've also had many unfortunate moments where I was mistreated by others just because they didn't think there was much to me as a result of my battle with mental illness. So, you may be wondering, how is it that I'm able to function the way I do, even with the mental illnesses that I've been diagnosed with and I'm here to answer that for you. At the start of my journey through mental health, there was so much I didn't know outside of going to see a counselor or therapist every week, and as life continued to happen, I came to realize how important it was for me to know what all of my options were because there was much more to navigating the mental health system than finding a good counselor and going to an appointment every week. Because I didn't know what was available to me, I suffered in silence out of fear at moments where I should have felt free enough to speak up and ask for what I needed. But I didn't know what to ask for. I didn't know who to ask.

That was until someone told me. It was in 2015, I was working in a call center for a company who was on the verge of terminating me for hanging up on several of my callers. At that time, my employer wasn't aware that I battled with severe anxiety and that the reason for the random hangups was because I would have a full anxiety attack while on the call and had no choice but to disconnect the line and get away from my desk as quickly as possible. Was I still going to counseling at that time? Yes, I was still going to counseling but there was more that I needed and before that moment, I didn't know what it was or how to ask for it. I was afraid of being judged if someone like my boss knew I had a mental health disability, so I came to work every day suffering and fighting to make it through my long shifts when I didn't have to. I was an undergrad at the time as well, suffering and barely passing my classes because I had a need that I didn't know how to ask for out of fear of being judged or treated differently. It was so bad, I was afraid to tell the therapist that I was seeing at the time because I was afraid that she might judge me too! It goes back to why I said having a good rapport and establishing trust with the therapist is important for moments such as this! So, back to this meeting I'm having with Human Resources and my supervisors about hanging up on my customers. I had a decision to make at that moment. I could either come clean about my disability and see what they could do to help me or remain silent out of fear and get fired for something that was truly outside of my control at the time. I took a deep breath and chose to tell them about my condition.

To my surprise, all of them were understanding and very supportive of me. They even said they were glad that I told them because they would not have known otherwise and would have hated to terminate an employee who was truly in need of additional help and support. I signed in relief and I was so glad I spoke up for myself and that I wasn't judged as I anticipated. At that moment, it was my first time learning about the Americans With Disabilities Act (ADA). ADA was a law that prohibited employers from discriminating against anyone based on their disability, race, gender and other factors. It also allowed for an employee who has a disability to receive reasonable workplace accommodations that would allow them to get the care they needed while still maintaining their employment with the company. The company I worked for at the time had an entire department and even a section on the main website that talked about the resources and ways that the company supported their associates who had physical and mental disabilities. My mind was blown because I had no idea that the company I was working for at that time had all of this available for me to use. Again, why it's important to know your options! So, I didn't lose my job and the company allowed me to take medical leave from the job to get the additional care I needed so that I could function in my role efficiently. That was also my first time learning that the Family Medical Leave Act (FMLA), Short Term Disability (STD) and Long Term Disability (LTD) was just for people with physical disabilities but mental as well.

When I took the leave, FMLA covered my time away from work so that I wouldn't be penalized by the company for missing so many days. The STD benefits allowed me to be paid a portion of my regular income while being out from work. LTD benefits would have only come into the picture as an option if I was out from work consecutively for longer than six months with the same condition. Thankfully, I was able to return to work within two three months and upon my return, my therapist gave me what I needed at that time to request workplace accommodations that would allow me to receive what I needed on the job while working. This helped me improve on my call efficiency to where I was no longer hanging up on callers and I was more efficient in my role overall up until the time that I chose to resign. In addition to that, I was also told about the Employee Assistance Program (EAP) that was provided to associates who worked for the company. EAP offered a variety of services including free short term counseling, financial guidance/assistance, legal assistance and many other resources as well. Even though I had a regular therapist and was not in needed of the short term counselor/therapist, the counselors who worked for EAP also served as a means of immediate support, meaning you're in a crisis of some kind at that very moment and would like someone to talk to for the moment until you attend your next session with your regular therapist.

Learning about these amazing resources that were available to someone like me who battled with mental illness helped me with every job I pursued and even with school. Learning this information helped me find out what the university I was attending at the time had to offer and I was able to find the counseling center on campus that offers counseling to students. I also learned about additional resources that provide testing accommodations to students with physical, mental and learning disabilities. I had the worst test anxiety and I was able to submit paperwork from my doctor that would allow me to take my exams outside of the class room and receive additional time in order to make sure that I remain calm during the test and not have an anxiety attack. Having those resources and the support of the counselors and other staff helped me stay in school and not give up. One thing I would encourage you to do as well when you're choosing a therapist, ask the therapist if they are willing to complete paperwork for you in the event that you're ever in need of services like the ones I've listed above such as time away from work under FMLA or Short Term Disability. Another service that is available are Social Security benefits which are funded through the state and local government. I know that at times you hear about these benefits for the elderly or someone who hurt themselves physically or has a physical disability, but it can also apply to those with mental illness if their condition is expected to prohibit them from working for a year or longer.

The reason that I said to ask the therapist if they're willing to do paperwork in the event that you need it is because with supporting documents from the therapist or doctor you're seeing, you would not be approved for any benefits outside of what's offered through EAP. Therapists are not required to complete paperwork for patients who take time away from work or have to quit working altogether due their condition, and there are some who won't do it no matter what. While the services that I've named are mandatory nor does it mean that what you have will ever lead to you needing those services, you want to be prepared just in case life ever happens to the point that you need them. The last thing you want is to realize in your time of need that you have a therapist who is unwilling to complete the documentation. That happened to me one time and I had to make a last minute change and work with a different counselor who was willing to do the paperwork for me. It was tough making such an abrupt switch like that, but I learned from that experience going forward to make sure that I asked this question to a therapist before agreeing to see them regularly. Everything that I've shared with you so far are all pieces of information that I learned through trial and error, it wasn't anything that was just given to me. That's part of what I mean about the responsibility part of your journey. There are some things that you won't know until you ask the right questions and do the research yourself, especially if you don't have a caretaker that does it for you.

Remember that nothing in this process is handed to you, it's given to the one who asks the question. I have a little more to share, but before I do, I want to give you an opportunity to process by journaling. How do you feel after what you've read so far about knowing your resources? Is it helping you on the journey that you're on now? Do you believe it will help you down the road? Did you learn anything new? Was there any part of what was stated that you already knew or had already received before? What was the experience like? Was it good or bad? What did you learn from it? Please take a moment to answer these questions and release as you process and pat yourself on the back because you're still here, and you're halfway to the finish line whether you realize it or not! Reading this book is part of your unique process and the journey that you're on to total healing and restoration in your mind, body and spirit.

____

____

____

Welcome back! I know I shared a lot and I pray that it wasn't too overwhelming for you. I also hope that you were able to release some by writing out your feelings after reading this chapter, and if you reached the end of the lines and realized you needed more space to write, that's okay. Having a journal of your own is key because sometimes you will have a lot to process and other moments you won't have as much. The point is you're processing and you're doing it with a purpose that is going to help you on your journey for days, months and years to come! There are two more components that I want to add when it comes to knowing your options, so that should it ever come up, you will remember that you read it here and you will know what to do in the moment.

I will start by encouraging you to take advantage of the National Suicide Prevention Lifeline by visiting www.988lifeline.org and also dialing 988 or 1-800-273-8255 should you be in a crisis or are just needing someone to talk to in the moment. You don't have to be suicidal to call this number or to visit the website. However, if you do think that you're going to harm yourself or someone, don't hesitate to dial 9-1-1 or proceed to your nearest emergency room. Dialing 9-1-1 doesn't mean you're in trouble with the police. You're simply getting help as quickly as possible. In the event that 9-1-1 is notified in this type of situation, the police will come just as a formality along with an ambulance to transport you to the nearest hospital or inpatient facility that will help you remain safe while working through your crisis. In Florida, they call it being Baker Acted if someone is transported to a hospital or behavioral health facility for a suicide attempt or a threat to commit suicide. It applies to someone who is having homicidal thoughts as well, meaning they want to harm another person. In case you're wondering, yes, I've been Baker Acted before. Both instances happened while I was living in Florida, which is where I'm originally from.

I'll actually talk more about what happened with that in my book entitled, *Grieving With Purpose*, which comes to Amazon on June 19, 2023. I shared that with you so that if you're reading this book and you're feeling this way or you've felt this way before, there's nothing for you to be ashamed about and you don't have to feel alone. Don't be afraid to follow the directives that I just gave if you're ever in that place, even if it's not your first time being in that place. As you continue your journey and get healed the right way, I can attest to the fact that you won't always feel this way and you will find purpose in life again. Will the enemy attempt to make you think otherwise? Yes, but the journey that you're on, the journey that I've taken is what will help you combat thoughts that are contrary to what God says about you and your purpose for being on this earth! The website I listed a moment ago offers a variety of resources and information concerning the importance of mental health, mental illness, and what resources are available in your area. Another additional resource is taking advantage of group therapy. I'll be honest with you by saying that the first time someone introduced the option of going to group therapy, I was totally against it because I didn't want to be around people talking about my battles with what I have, even though I knew the people in the group were battling just like me. I just didn't think I could handle anything outside of one-on- one counseling, so I stuck to that and my therapist allowed me to continue with what I was comfortable with.

That is another sign that you have a good therapist is when they make suggestions and don't force you to accept their suggestions, but allow you to make the decision for yourself. Now, I will tell you that after years of saying I would never go to group therapy, I ended up having a change of heart with going in the summer of 2021 when I was on a leave of absence from work. The therapist I was seeing at the time suggested it and I said I was interested until we both found out that the insurance company was not going to pay out Short Term Disability benefits if I didn't agree to the six week group therapy sessions. So, I unfortunately had no choice but to say yes and I went through six weeks of group therapy. In the beginning,

I had an attitude about being there but after a couple of days, I had a change of heart and I started enjoying the sessions more than I thought I would. By the end of the sessions, I was seen as a leader among the group that the other people in the group could relate to and be inspired by. That meant so much to me and I realized it was all worth it. While I don't believe it is something I would try again, I am glad I at least had the chance to try it once because it turned out to offer me a lot of tools that I still use today. For example, we did a lot of breathing exercises in those sessions and breathing wasn't something I was used to and I didn't see the point of it at first. But I did it and I found that it worked. Those very breathing techniques are what help me now when I start to feel anxiety build or if there's a moment where I've had a panic attack.

Breathing makes the difference in how long it takes me to come down from it, so I said all of that to say, don't knock it until you try it. But never feel pressured to do it either. Now you may be wondering why it was that I was required to do something that should have been optional, and I am getting ready to explain that in just a moment as we prepare to wrap up this chapter. Before I bring out the last point for this chapter, I want to give you another opportunity to release through journaling. I know that for some people, talking about suicide can be triggering and a very touch subject for some. If it was for you, I want to give you the chance to release that before we continue so that you're not overwhelmed the rest of the journey. I'll make it simple by asking you these questions as a way to help you as you write what you're feeling on this particular about suicide and seeing life worth living. Have you ever had thoughts of suicide before? Has someone you know ever had thoughts of suicide before? If so, how long ago was your last thought? When you had the thought, what did you do about it? Have you ever attempted suicide before? Has someone you know ever attempted suicide before? If someone you know attempted suicide, did they survive their attempt? If so, was that person able to get the help they needed? If that person didn't survive, I first offer my condolences and I am deeply sorry for your loss. How long ago did it happen? How have you processed such a tragic loss as this? Are you still processing? Are you currently seeking therapy or plan to seek therapy to deal with the loss of this loved one?

Welcome back once again to the journey, and if you needed some time to process this last entry, I totally understand. There is nothing wrong with stopping and coming back to it later, just as long as you don't give up. Remember, I told you at the beginning that there were parts of this healing journey that would not be easy. But if you're reading this, it means that you're still pushing through and I am very proud of you! Keep going and keep winning! You're almost there, you're almost to the finish line! The last thing I want to talk about is knowing your options and your rights from a legal perspective.

As much as we would like for everyone to abide by the laws that are in place and do right by those of us who battle with mental illness, experience in this life will teach you that not everyone is as nice as we would like for them to be. Some are mean to the point that they will use verbal, mental and even physical abuse to attack or further tear down someone with mental illness because they like being a bully who can overpower someone they see as weak. Again, there are people who will have a false perception about the weight of who you are by assuming that you're limited to your disability. Knowing how to fight is good but knowing how to fight the right way is even better, and the most productive in the end. Have you ever been mistreated by someone as a result of your battle with mental illness? If so, write about that experience on the lines below. How did it make you feel? Did you tell anyone what happened or did you keep it to yourself?

If you took the challenge and wrote down the time(s) where you were mistreated as a result of having a disability, I am proud of you and I apologize on behalf of any one who mistreated you or abused you in any way. If you weren't quite ready to write about it, that is okay too and I am still proud. You're still healing! There are some experiences that may be hard for us to release outside of therapy, even when simply writing it down and that is okay. You will release what happened when the time is right for you and I apologize on behalf of those who mistreated and abused you as well. It wasn't right and at no point did you deserve to experience what happened to you.

Many years ago, it was more common to see people who had various types of disabilities to be isolated from the general public in certain environments to avoid them being teased or mistreated by those who did not suffer from a disability. But over time, things changed and it became common to see certain spaces where people with and without a disability were gathered collectively and the goal was to allow a level of coexistence that wouldn't single out someone or a group of people who have a disability by giving everyone the same opportunity. For example, when I finished my Associate of Arts degree and transferred to a university, I did work study for a short period of time. One of the departments I was assigned to worked with students who had disabilities, and it was there where I learned that these students were no longer shut away in classrooms separate from the rest of the students, but they were allowed to register for the same classes as everyone else and it became a norm to see students with disabilities in regular college courses.

I don't know if the expectations for them were different or not, but the point was, the university was making an attempt to bridge a gap by making sure that everyone was allowed the same learning opportunities regardless of disability. It all ties back to the rights that people who live with disabilities have. Now, I shared at the beginning how knowing what resources are available to you is important because what you don't know could cause you to miss out on opportunities that you're rightfully entitled to have. Now I want to share on what to do in the event that you find yourself in a situation where you believe an injustice has been done against you that should result in legal action being taken. Every situation is different and if you believe that this is something that an attorney will need to get involved

with, and if you don't already have an attorney, call
your State Bar for the state that you live in or the
local Legal Aid depending on what city you reside in.
There you would explain your situation and the
service offered would help you find an attorney that
can help you with your potential case. There is also a
website called Avvo, which allows you to pose
questions to lawyers in your area and receive
answers that will potentially help you determine if
you have a case or not against the other party. Now,
everything I've said so far is done by simply Google
searching. You're also welcome to tell your therapist
and receive a directive on how to go about getting
legal help for your situation.

If mistreatment or discrimination due to disability
happens at your job, you would want to look up the
Equal Employment Opportunity Commission (EEOC)
for your state and start a claim with their office so
that you can schedule a hearing with one of their
representatives. Lastly, if the complaint you want to
file is against a therapist, counselor, doctor,
psychiatrist, etc., you're still allowed to contact Legal
Aid or the State Bar for assistance. You can also
retrieve the license number of the therapist online
and use it as a reference to file a complaint with the
State Board that they received their license through.
While there's no guarantee that anything can actually
be done, it never hurts to try because it allows you to
find your own voice and no longer be controlled by
those who don't think there's much to your life as a
result of your disability. You can't control what

people think, but you can control how much you decide to take by choosing to use your rights and finding your voice by not being afraid to speak up for yourself.

Know Your Options

While therapy isn't for everyone, there are many options available to choose from for those that it is for. What I mean is that there is more than one kind of therapist and in this chapter, I want to break them down for you so that as you choose who you're going to see, you will know how to research for you're in need of and never assume that you have to settle because of what you don't know. If you're currently in therapy or you're one who has been to therapy before and are thinking about going back, this chapter can still be of great help when it comes to deciding or even making sure that what you have currently is truly the best fit for the journey that you're on.

I will start by saying that **if you are ever in a state of crisis where you intend to harm yourself or someone else, please dial 9-1-1 or proceed to your nearest emergency room. You can also reach out to the National Suicide Prevention Lifeline at 800-273-8255 or just by dialing or texting 9-8-8. You can also visit suicidepreventionlifeline.org** for more information on what to do in a crisis as well as information on finding additional mental health resources in your area. Below is a list of the different types of counselors/therapists that you will potentially come across when searching for the right one. Knowing specifics about the licensing of your potential therapist is important because it will ensure that you choose someone who is capable of addressing your specific condition. In addition to what is listed here in this book, you can also find this information and more online at several websites including but not limited to allpsychologyschools.com, psychologytoday.com, verywellhealth.com, betterhelp.com and psychologyschoolguide.net.

Psychiatrist
Psychoanalyst
Psychiatric Nurse
Psychotherapist
Mental Health Counselor
Family & Marriage Counselor
Rehabilitation Counseling
Guidance & Career Counseling
Nurse Practitioner

While these are not all of them, these are the names of a few that I believe will help you on your search. In addition to having an understanding of what type of therapist will work best for you, it is also important to know your options when it comes to having the necessary resources to care for yourself in the event that you need to get medication, apply for benefits or take any form of medical leave from your place of employment. While this is not something that happens to everyone, sometimes situations happen where your symptoms become severe to the point that you have to take medication and/or take time away from work and apply for benefits that will support you for the time that you're out of work. Setting this up is no different than having insurance, you don't wait until you're in a situation to get it, you prepare by having it in place at all times. I will start by encouraging you to look up the Americans with Disabilities Act (ADA) on ada.gov. On this website, you will be able to read the definition as well as how this law protects you as a person who battles with mental illness. In case you're wondering, yes, having a mental illness also qualifies as a disability and it's part of why this law was put in place. The information on site will be useful whether it's your first time going to therapy, you're returning to therapy or you're currently seeking therapy.

I will continue by starting with those who are new to therapy or are starting it for the first time. If you're working a job, ask your Human Resources department or benefits department if you qualify for medical leave under the Family Medical Leave Act (FMLA). Some employers have a separate bank of medical leave aside from FMLA because of the rules and laws that apply, but it's important that you know your options either way so that you're prepared should you need time away from work as a result of your mental illness. The Department of Labor (DOL) website at dol.gov can provide more information on FMLA, who qualifies and how to make sure it's available to you in the event that you need it. In addition to that, find out if your employer offers Short Term Disability (STD) and/or Long Term Disability (LTD) benefits to their associates. Most of the time, employers provide this information to their associates when they first start working during onboarding or at some point during your on the job training. The Georgia.gov website at dps.georgia.gov provides detailed information on both in addition to the information given by the employer should they have it as an option. In short, FMLA is what covers you for the duration of time that you're out from work and it means that your employer won't penalize you for the number of days missed. STD benefits pays you a percentage of your salary for the time that you're out for up to six months.

After six months, LTD benefits would go into effect if available. If LTD benefits weren't available, your employer may use any Paid Time Off (PTO) that you have available or they may have another alternative based on the company's procedures. Should you max out the time allowed for LTD benefits, speak to your therapist prior to your deadline for next step instructions because you will potentially have to apply for disability benefits through the state. Lastly, I'll mention that when finding a therapist, it doesn't hurt to ask them if they are willing to complete the required paperwork that would be needed to process your claim for benefits if you took time off from work due to mental illness. While most of them are willing, it's best to ask because it is not required that a therapist complete the paperwork for their patient, even if they are the ones suggesting that the patient take time from work. They can document that you were told to be out of work, but completing paperwork for your employer that allows you to file a claim for benefits is not mandatory. So, it is important to keep that in mind when deciding who you will see because without that paperwork, you would not be able to receive what you need when you take time off, especially when it comes to getting paid if you're approved to receive STD benefits. Unless your employer has a different method, most of the time you're paid at the same time of the month that you're paid your regular pay. So, if you're typically paid two times a month on the 15th and the last day of the month, then your benefits will be paid out on the 15th and the last day of the month. If you're paid every two weeks, your benefits will be paid out every two weeks.

Delays in submitting all required paperwork for processing can delay your benefits. It doesn't mean you won't receive it, but you could potentially receive it on the next pay cycle. For example, if I get paid every two weeks and I'm not paid on time, I will have to wait to receive payment the next pay date and that is only if all paperwork is received and correct. When it comes to where you file your claim, that solely depends on the provider that the company is partnered with. The process for receiving benefits while out from work can be very strenuous and there is a lot that goes into it. The more you know going in, the smoother the process will be and this is why it's important to do your research and know your options so that you're prepared in the event that something happens where you have to take time away from work. Another resource that is usually available through most employers is the Employee Assistance Program (EAP). This program offers short term counseling, immediate support, legal, financial and many other resources to all associates. It can be of help to you at any time whether you're taking time away from work or not.

Please remember that this is not something that happens to everyone and if you're able to work without ever needing to take time away, that is a plus and it just means that you have your resources in place should anything change. If you work for a company that does not offer these services and you're at a place where you may need to take time off from work due to mental illness, I would strongly encourage you to speak to your therapist about your concerns and allow them to give you directions on what to do next.

If you're not working and you don't anticipate being able to go to work for twelve months or longer as a result of your mental illness, talk to your therapist immediately to ask for their support in applying for disability benefits which is also known as social security. There is paperwork and documentation needed from your therapist in order for your application to be processed. This is another example of why having a supportive therapist that you have established trust and a good rapport with is key because you never know what turns you will take on the road to healing and wholeness. On the lines below, please write down what you learned after reading the information in this chapter. How much did you already know prior to reading? Was this your first time hearing any of it? What will being prepared in this regard look like for you after reading this chapter?

Work Therapy!

After you find the right therapist and educate yourself on the many options that are available to you before, during and even after your process, it's now time to properly go through the process with your therapist with the understanding that you're not waiting for therapy to work, but you're going to work therapy! Everything you've read up to this point was for this very moment of going from the mindset of worrying that this thing we call therapy might not work to learning how to work this thing we call therapy! This is what you want to remember as you go through your journey in therapy or even a short term approach with counseling. Make sure your expectations are realistic by remembering what the mental health system was designed to do!

Most people who reject therapy and say that it doesn't work either never tried it and they're making assumptions or they tried it with unrealistic expectations of the system and assumed it was ineffective as a result of it. While therapy, counseling and other components of using mental health services are designed as a means of support, the overall system itself was created to help you get to a place where you function in life while coping with what you have been diagnosed with on your own.

In order for that to happen, your therapist or counselor will challenge you to do things to help prepare you for that stage of your journey. It is important that you trust the process as I told you before and do as you're told, even if what they are asking you to do doesn't make sense. Most of the time when you have that moment of questioning what you're being told, you will gain an understanding of why it had to be done once you do it and see the effectiveness of it. But of course keep in mind that what you're challenged to do by your therapist should be legal practices that fall within all guidelines of the law and the Code of Ethics! For example, a therapist should never use sexual favors or even conversations during sessions as part of a treatment plan for their patient. That along with any other illegal practices or even unlicensed practicing from a person claiming to be therapist should be reported immediately to the State Board that the therapist is licensed through as well as the police!

Outside of that, trust your therapist and trust the process by having an open mind to take the necessary steps that will help you leave therapy equipped with what you need to move forward with your life. An unrealistic expectation is when you come to therapy expecting your therapist to *"fix you"* or when you wait for a certain feeling to assure you that you're okay. Therapy does not work that way. Your therapist is not your healer but they are there to help you take the necessary steps needed to heal. That being said, you're just as much a part of this journey as they are and if you remember that along the way, you will be very successful in therapy and you will ultimately leave knowing how to *"work therapy"* by effectively applying what you gain from therapy into your everyday life. Even if you're not much of a writer, keep a journal with you throughout the process. When you're expressing yourself in your journal, it doesn't have to be grammatically or politically correct by any means! Write it how you feel it! The release will help you as well, especially during the moments that are the most intense. For example, the first time I ever talked about being molested at age seven, I had to not only talk through that process but journal through it as well. I had gone nearly thirteen years without ever speaking about it to anyone and as happy as I was to finally be in a safe place to release it, it wasn't easy to do after carrying something as traumatic as that for so many years.

Now if you can, turn to your journal throughout your process before turning to social media. Your social media is yours and I can't tell you what to do with it, but venting your emotional pain and distress on social media platforms expecting support from those who follow you is very risky and something that is not encouraged. As I told you earlier, having support is necessary on the journey, but you have to have the right kind of support and there is no guarantee that everyone who sees what you post on Facebook will be as supportive as you want them to be. I've seen people I knew personally who battled with mental illness post on social media and received some of the harshest and most hurtful responses from people that knew them. There are even unfortunate cases where unhealthy and harmful interactions on social media has driven people young and old to commit suicide. As you go through your process in therapy, it is important to remain focused and be mindful of what you say on these platforms. If you're having a moment where you feel that journaling is not enough, don't hesitate to call the Suicide Prevention Line or your EAP for immediate support, seven days a week, anytime of the day or night. Another option if you're a student is the after hours number through the counseling center at the college or university that you attend, even if you're an online student. There are usually counselors there who will offer immediate support and provide feedback with whatever you're dealing with at that very moment.

Of course it's not meant to serve as a counseling or therapy session, just support to help you until you're able to see your therapist again. As I speak on being mindful of who you talk to before, during and even after your journey, I would also encourage you to take this same approach with your employer if you are working. By law, you're not required to make your employer aware of your mental health condition or diagnosis. I notice on job applications, there are companies that will ask you if you have a disability or if you've ever had one. While it does usually allow you the option of declining to answer, understand that you are allowed to choose not to respond and not at any point do you have to reveal your diagnosis. So, you may wonder how this would work if you were in need of time off due to your diagnosis. Depending on the company you work for, there are some who have on-site nurses and doctors to assist associates with getting the care they need should they need to take time off from work for a medical reason. Even though their licensing and legal obligation to keep your medical history and any knowledge they have of your diagnosis confidential, you're still not required to go into details about it if you're not comfortable. There are ways to use verbiage that doesn't reveal anything to your employer about your condition outside of the fact that you need time off for a medical reason. But should you decide to tell your employer for whatever reason about your diagnosis, be very careful and know your rights as well as your options legally should there be any level of harassment, abuse, retaliation or discrimination that takes place as a result of what you reveal about having a mental illness or a disability. That plays a part in ADA law as well.

Another important factor is keeping your appointments and remaining consistent. If the therapist wants you to see them once a week, every other week, etc., keep those appointments because the consistency helps and allows you to grow from the place you started. Now I understand that life happens and there could be an occasion where you have to miss an appointment and that is okay as long as it doesn't become a habit. Just be sure as a courtesy, to cancel within enough time for your therapist to fill your appointment slot for another client of theirs who may be waiting to be scheduled. Most therapists will outline in the initial paperwork that you sign what the policy is for cancellations. It is important to know what that is because there are some therapists who will charge a fee if you fail to cancel or reschedule your appointment within the time frame of your appointment that is set. The next thing is if you're taking medication. Please, please please, take your medication as prescribed by your psychiatrist or doctor! For example, if you're supposed to take the medication one time a day, make sure that once you start it you remain consistent with it. Never skip a day, even if it means reminding yourself by setting an alarm in your phone or buying a container that allows you to put each pill for each day inside of it so that you don't skip a dose. While not all medications have the same instructions for how you take them, inconsistencies in taking your meds as prescribed can potentially intensify your symptoms and ultimately become ineffective.

This means you would be taking the meds and they're no longer working. I've met people who only take their medication when they feel an episode of anxiety or their mood shifting starting to happen and then when they feel better, they stop taking it. That's not how taking this kind of medication works. You must be consistent and if or when you reach the place that you're ready to stop taking the medication, there is a protocol of safety to follow for that to. Don't ever abruptly stop taking your meds because you don't feel that you need them anymore. If you feel that way, great! But allow the same doctor or psychiatrist who prescribed you the medication to help safely wean you off of it so that your body properly adjusts to no longer having the medication in its system. Talking about my own journey, I will be honest with you and say that when I stopped taking medication back in November 2021, it wasn't done the right way. That's why I'm telling you how important it is to be sure that you allow a doctor or psychiatrist to help you. I was taking a medication at the time called Celexa for anxiety and mood disorders and it was working fine. I took it every day and I felt good, but I reached a point where I no longer wanted to take it and out of fear that the psychiatrist would not allow me to stop, I decided to stop on my own thinking that I would be okay. But I went through extreme withdrawal when I stopped for a few weeks with my symptoms intensifying to the point that I thought I wanted to kill myself. Thankfully, I did not hurt myself or anyone else and it's been nearly two years since I stopped and I haven't felt better!

Now please don't think that because I managed to get through that intense moment that it means you should do the same, please work with your doctor or psychiatrist if you're taking medication and are wanting to stop them. I will also add that should anything happen where you're about to run out of medication and you don't have a refill pending, it is okay to visit a local clinic or urgent care center to request a temporary prescription from the doctor while you wait for a new refill from your psychiatrist. Most doctors will do it for you once and in the event that one decides not to help you, let your therapist and psychiatrist know before completely running out of medication so you can be instructed on what to do next. Lastly, remain consistent in following the instructions and challenges given for you to do while in therapy. There will be some things that only have to be done that once, but there will be other things that you're told to do on a more consistent basis to help you on your journey and the more you follow those instructions, the better it will be for you while in therapy and even after. Your ability to see therapy work for you is all up to you and it is possible when you remain open, available and ready from the start of the process with your therapist to the end of it. On the lines below, write your plan for working therapy in a way that allows you to succeed and accomplish your goals while in therapy? If you're ready in therapy, what were the goals that you set for yourself going into it? Or did you set any? After reading this chapter, has this information added value to your goals or has it helped you start thinking about what you ultimately want to accomplish while in therapy?

Continue the Journey!

You may have heard the old saying that goes, "every good thing must come to an end." I'm not talking about the last chapter of this book because my goal is for this book to always serve as a tool and a guide for you at every stage of your journey before, during and after! I mentioned this quote because even though therapy is for long-term care, it does not mean that you're supposed to remain in it for the rest of your life. There is a process that you're meant to walk through that helps you to graduate and reach a place where you no longer need therapy because you have grown and healed to a place where you can take the tools and information gained throughout the process to continue the journey of this thing we call life. I have mentioned throughout this book how important it is to write down your goals for what you're looking to accomplish in therapy. Well for this challenge, write down the goals that you're looking to accomplish with your personal life endeavors once you reach the end of therapy.

Understand that these goals don't have to be anything extravagant. It can be as simple as making a commitment to go outside and get some fresh air every day or a few times a week if you were typically used to staying home all the time. That's something I've become more accustomed to doing for myself because I am a homebody. Being a homebody isn't bad, but one thing therapy taught me is how to have proper balance of when it's okay to be home and when it's beneficial for my journey to enjoy the outdoors. So, that's one example of what I mean when it comes to expectations that you set for yourself because it is not about how you started but how you finish and how you will continue!

Now if after you've stopped going to therapy, you feel the need to do a check-in appointment with your therapist, that is okay to do as well and understand that this chapter is not directing anyone to stop therapy at this point or any other. You stay as long as it takes, just be productive! I added this chapter because I know from my own experience that once you're assured of the effectiveness of the work you have put in, you will find yourself before you know it at a place where you no longer need to continue going to therapy the way you once did. This is not a process that you have to rush through because no one's process is the same. It's all about how you move through it, how you feel as you move through it and the results that you're seeing as a result of those moves. I would definitely encourage you to express these goals to your therapist so they can make helpful suggestions for you as well that will help you during the transition when the time comes. I would also encourage you not to be afraid when the time for transition comes, especially if you realize that it came at a moment that you didn't anticipate. That's what happened to me! When I first realized my season of therapy was up, it took a minute for me to adjust because I had been doing it for so long before finally getting it right and making it work. I went back to my therapist and they gave me very helpful tools and tips that helped me transition gracefully without fear of the unknown. It took some time but within about three to four months, I was adapting in my life better than I ever had before.

I had my blueprint and plan for managing my symptoms of anxiety and mood disorders, and I was also able to see how much healing had taken place from past trauma, and I continued to take the necessary steps to continue in the progress I made throughout therapy. You will one day be able to do the same and as you do it, you will have the same desire I did to help others come through their process as well. You may write books like I have or you may start a blog, an online course or become a motivational speaker to your target audience. The possibilities truly are endless as you continue the journey with the understanding that you're no longer bound to what happened to you in your past and that you're free to live and capable of any opportunity that life has for you to take hold of! It's all about reaching up and grabbing it for yourself and ultimately remembering how far you've truly come and that greater days are ahead! Stay encouraged and stay the course! I believe in you and I wish you well in every endeavor! If this book has blessed you, I encourage you to leave a thought provoking review on Amazon that will push another person out there who is fighting the same war to invest in this book and get what they need to start the process and finish it strong knowing that therapy worked for them because they learned how to work therapy!

Sometimes growth can feel traumatic. It's not always pretty but it's necessary.
~Ricky Holloway